No-Code Apps

No-Code Apps

Apps

ServiceNow Special Edition

by Chuck Tomasi
and Brad Tilton

No-Code Apps For Dummies®, ServiceNow Special Edition

Published by
John Wiley & Sons, Inc.
111 River St.
Hoboken, NJ 07030-5774
www.wiley.com

ISBN 978-1-119-65383-7 (pbk); ISBN 978-1-119-65384-4 (ebk)

Manufactured in the United States of America

C10013447_082719

For general information on our other products and services, or how to create a custom *For Dummies* book for your business or organization, please contact our Business Development Department in the U.S. at 877-409-4177, contact info@dummies.biz, or visit www.wiley.com/go/custompub. For information about licensing the *For Dummies* brand for products or services, contact BrandedRights&Licenses@Wiley.com.

Publisher's Acknowledgments

Some of the people who helped bring this book to market include the following:

Project Editor: Elizabeth Kuball

Executive Editor: Steve Hayes

Editorial Manager: Rev Mengle

Business Development Representative: Karen Hattan

Production Editor: Magesh Elangovan

Special Help: Donna Tomasi

Table of Contents

INTRODUCTION.. 1

About This Book 1
Foolish Assumptions.. 2
Icons Used in This Book.. 2
Beyond This Book.. 3

CHAPTER 1: **Beginning with a Plan** 5

Before You Build: Asking the Right Questions..................... 5
Making Permanent Decisions 8
Choosing between a scoped app and a global app.......... 8
Deciding where to build your app 8
Naming your app 9
Naming your tables and fields 9
Identifying the Prerequisites for Building an App 10

CHAPTER 2: **Storing Your Information**................................ 11

Getting to Know Your Toolbox.. 11
Making Choices about Your Tables....................................... 12
Extending a table 13
Uploading a spreadsheet.. 15
Creating a table from scratch 16
Creating Fields 16
Choice fields versus reference fields............................. 17
Field attributes 19
Putting the Finishing Touches on Your Tables.................... 19
Choosing a table label 20
Picking a table name 20
Making your table extensible 20
Auto-numbering your records 21
Managing access 21

CHAPTER 3: **Creating Amazing Experiences** 23

Using Forms and Lists.. 24
Taking It Mobile 26
Working with Workspace.. 27
Getting the Ultimate Control with Service Portal 28
Using Reports and Dashboards... 29

CHAPTER 4: **Logic and Workflow**... 33

Building Dynamic Form Logic 33

Validating and Simplifying Updates with Business Rules............. 34

Controlling Your App with Flow Designer 36

Connecting to Third-Party Systems with IntegrationHub............. 38

Using Notifications to Communicate 39

CHAPTER 5: **More No-Code Capabilities**.................................. 41

Building a Chatbot.. 41

Components of Virtual Agent 42

Benefits of Virtual Agent 42

Testing Your App 44

Components of the Automated Test Framework 44

Benefits of the Automated Test Framework 45

Sending Surveys 45

Offering Self-Paced Onscreen Training 46

Improving Standard Menus 47

CHAPTER 6: **Ten Tips for No-Code App Development**................ 49

Making a Plan.. 49

Naming Apps, Tables, and Fields...................................... 49

Considering Some Common Personas and Roles.......................... 50

Using Good Form and List Layout..................................... 50

Taking Advantage of Different Field Types........................ 50

Avoiding Deleting Records 51

Testing Your App 51

Getting Familiar with the Commonly Used Tables...................... 51

Limiting the Number of Records Retrieved in a Report 51

Working with Your Developers 52

APPENDIX: **Resources**.. 53

Introduction

Many organizations have a priority to digitize their processes. This means getting away from the legacy ad-hoc processes and getting a system of record that can drive productivity. The reality is that your IT group likely doesn't have the bandwidth to get to everyone's project, especially when digitizing your process may not "move the needle" all that much. The good news is, you can reduce IT workload by empowering "citizen developers" (or, as we like to call them, "builders") with the tools and processes needed to build their own applications (or apps) on the Now Platform from ServiceNow. The Now Platform provides a single mobile and web app development environment, allowing people with limited to no coding experience to quickly build business apps that power the digital transformation.

About This Book

This book explain how anyone can automate, extend, and build digital workflow apps across the organization using the Now Platform and several key, no-code capabilities. *No-Code Apps For Dummies* consists of six chapters that explore the following:

- » Creating a plan for your app (Chapter 1)
- » Basic data setup techniques (Chapter 2)
- » Creating an amazing experience for your app's users (Chapter 3)
- » Building logic to unlock productivity (Chapter 4)
- » Some additional no-code Now Platform capabilities to add to your app (Chapter 5)
- » No-code tips and tricks from the experts (Chapter 6)

Foolish Assumptions

We made some assumptions about you, our reader, when we were writing this book. Mainly, we assume the following:

» **You're a subject matter expert in your role.** You may be a process owner, specialist, or senior member of a team. Whether you're in accounting, legal, marketing, or the safety department, you know your stuff!

» **You're in an organization that is changing.** Business requirements evolve. Either you're fortunate enough to have to scale quickly or you're being asked "to do more with less." Either way, yesterday's techniques and technology just aren't effective today.

» **You don't create applications for a living.** You didn't go to school for a computer science degree and you've likely never written any code.

» **You recognize that you have ad-hoc processes.** These processes may use email, spreadsheets, or perhaps even paper (gasp!). You also recognize that these processes could be improved with digital transformation.

Icons Used in This Book

Throughout this book, we use icons in the margin to draw your attention to certain kinds of information. Here's what the icons mean:

REMEMBER

This book is a reference, which means you don't have to memorize it and there won't be a test on Friday. But when we tell you something so important that you should commit it to memory, we use the Remember icon.

TIP

Whenever you see the Tip icon, you can be sure to find some useful nugget of information that will save you time or money or just make your life a little easier — at least when it comes to developing apps!

WARNING

The Warning icon alerts you to things that could cause you big headaches. Think of these as orange cones in the road, warning you about an open manhole cover. Sure, you could ignore them, but you might take a nasty fall.

TECHNICAL STUFF

Every once in a while, our inner geeks come out, and we tell you information that's a bit technical. If you're short on time, you can skip anything marked with the Technical Stuff icon — it isn't absolutely necessary to understanding the subject at hand. But if you're a geek, too, you might find these pieces of information especially interesting!

Beyond This Book

This book focuses on the conceptual steps to building an app and points out many no-code capabilities on the Now Platform to enable you to build those apps, but we don't have room for detailed "how-to" information. If you want even more information, check out ServiceNow's annual Knowledge Conference (https://knowledge.servicenow.com). The CreatorCon event at Knowledge contains many hands-on workshops tailored to you, the builder. Also, try working with your ServiceNow account team to hold an Innovation Workshop in your area. Finally, you can also use this book's appendix to learn more about the concepts covered in these pages.

Chapter **1**

Beginning with a Plan

You probably wouldn't head out on a road trip without at least a general idea of how to get where you're going — at least not if you want to get there anytime soon! Planning is essential in life, as well as in app development.

In this chapter, you learn the importance of planning. You discover some key questions to ask yourself and find topics to consider to ensure you achieve the best possible outcome for your app.

Before You Build: Asking the Right Questions

Your answers to the following questions will help to determine how you can best utilize the Now Platform features to build an app that maximizes business value for your organization:

> » **What are the goals, objectives, and outputs of your app? In other words, what business problem are you trying to solve?** Without a specific business objective, you'll have difficulty measuring the success of your app or justifying its continued use within the organization.

Before you start building, begin with the end in mind. Understanding and visualizing (virtually or on a whiteboard) your desired solution helps determine the remaining steps in building your app. Often, the outputs are the drivers for the inputs. If you're trying to speed up a process, for example, knowing your output metrics can help make clear what to measure. If you're managing assets, perhaps cost and location are more important than the minute details of each item. Identifying your goals and objectives will ensure you can manage conversations with key stakeholders so that your app is specifically addressing your desired business outcomes.

Here's an example of a clear objective: *Reduce the time it takes to route and approve time-off requests from five days to less than one day.*

>> **Are you taking a spreadsheet and turning it into an app in ServiceNow, or does the app exist somewhere else?** This question impacts your approach for building the app because there are different tools within the Now Platform to support your efforts.

Take this opportunity to review and revise your process. Too many times, processes are dictated by limitations of legacy tools. Don't cripple your new app by trying to make it work like the old one did. After all, if the old app were perfect, you wouldn't be building a new one.

>> **Who will be using your app?** Identifying your target audience has a direct impact on the features your app will provide, the data it will capture, and the interface you need to provide for your app.

>> **Do you want everyone to have the same ability to see and edit fields, or will some people need more or less access than others?** Security is a significant and ever growing concern in most organizations, so identifying who has access to what during the planning stage is a critical step in app development.

>> **What will the users do with the app?** Will they be providing information, collecting information, routing information, requesting information, looking up information, and/or collaborating on information? Identifying these actions establishes the features and functions you'll need to build into your app.

>> **Where is the data coming from?** One of the most common conclusions is that data will be entered by people. Some data

(like users, departments, and locations) may already be available within your ServiceNow instance. You may also find that you require data from an external data source that you need to import.

TIP

When necessary, leverage existing data sources to avoid data entry duplication and make sure your app has the data it needs to meet its business objectives.

» **How will people interact with your app? Will they use computers or mobile devices or both?** Understanding how people access your app impacts how your app will function. Will they take action with a swipe of a finger or click of a mouse or both?

» **Can you walk through one or more example use cases or scenarios?** Walking through an example use case, or "day in the life of," is a great way to discover an app's requirements.

» **Is there an existing app in ServiceNow that already does (most of) what you need?** Why reinvent the wheel? If there is an app that does what you need, or close to it, look at the possibility of using or extending that existing app.

REMEMBER

Many organizations think that their processes are unique when they're actually pretty similar to what other organizations have done before. Take advantage of that similarity!

» **How will your stakeholders need to report in your app?** If your app is meeting a business purpose, you may want to provide reports showing usage, adoption, and key business objectives associated with the app.

» **Is this a good fit?** Not every app idea makes for a good fit on the Now Platform. In general, your app is a good fit for the Now Platform if it involves

- Simple forms
- Task management
- Repeatable processes
- Excel-driven processes
- Request fulfillment
- Third-party integration
- Orchestrating multiple systems

If your app involves the following, the Now Platform probably isn't what you need:

- Unstructured data

- Graphics processing or streaming video or audio
- Unrepeatable processes

Make sure your app is a good fit for ServiceNow before you start building.

TIP

Making Permanent Decisions

When you're building an app, you'll inevitably take some steps that are irreversible. You need to be aware of what these irreversible steps are so you can plan in advance and make the right moves.

Choosing between a scoped app and a global app

When you create an app, you can choose to create it in a private scope (called a *scoped app*) or in the global scope (called a *global app*). Scoped apps get extra functionality for managing development, deploying the app, and data security.

TIP

By default, all apps are created in a private scope. ServiceNow recommends that citizen developers or builders work with scoped apps.

REMEMBER

After an app is created, you can't switch from a scoped app to a global app or vice versa.

Deciding where to build your app

Proof of concept (PoC) app builds can be built in a personal developer instance that you get from the developer portal (http://developer.servicenow.com). These instances are named something like dev12345.service-now.com.

WARNING

You can rebuild PoC apps, but do not import them from your personal developer instance into your organization's instance. There is information included with your app that indicates where it was built. If you bring the app over from your personal developer instance, life will be a lot harder when you try to get your app in to production.

TIP

Apps that your organization will actually use (for example, production apps) should be created in your organization's developer instance so the app can follow your organization's testing and deployment process. See your ServiceNow System Administrator for more details about which instance to use for an app that will eventually be deployed to your organization's production instance.

Naming your app

Based on your app's display name, the Now Platform suggests a default (internal) name called the *app scope*. The app scope will be in the form of x_[*company code*]_[*app_name*], like this: x_acme_legal_request.

REMEMBER

Everything you create within your app will inherit that scope name, so it's important to think about what it should be when you start. The display name of the app can always be changed, but the scope name cannot.

Naming your tables and fields

After your app is created, you'll most likely be creating new tables and fields for it. Tables and fields have both labels (displayed in your browser and mobile user interface, or UI) as well as internal database names. Labels can be edited and even translated later, but internal database names can only be edited at creation time.

TIP

For tables, a label like "Safety issues" may produce a name of x_snc_safety_safety_issues. For consistency, use singular table names. ServiceNow will automatically produce plural labels where needed. Also, avoid redundancy in the table name; x_snc_safety_issue proves a lot less troublesome than x_snc_safety_safety_issue when you're maintaining your app down the road.

TIP

Similarly, you may be tempted to build fields with verbose labels, such as "How many widgets do you require?" This translates into a field named how_many_widgets_do_you_require_ (because spaces and symbols become underscores in the database). This field label is troublesome for users because it may not be displayed as expected and developers will have to deal with an awful field name in their scripts. Instead, consider just labeling the field "Widgets" to create a field called widgets.

REMEMBER

You can always relabel, but you can't rename. If you want to provide a longer description, ServiceNow offers hover-over tips and clickable links.

Identifying the Prerequisites for Building an App

Before building your app, you need the following:

» **A ServiceNow instance:** You can get one for free at the ServiceNow developer portal (http://developer.servicenow.com).

» **An admin or delegated developer role in that ServiceNow instance:** A delegated developer role is a role with fewer privileges than the admin role, but it still allows for app development.

TIP

Don't let the name *developer* throw you off. The ServiceNow developer portal has something to offer all skill levels when it comes to solving real business problems using the Now Platform. Here are some of the things you can find there, completely free of charge:

» **A personal developer instance (PDI):** You can use your own instance running the supported ServiceNow release of your choice. Use your admin-level access to configure the instance and make amazing apps.

» **Early access:** Developer program members get access to the latest ServiceNow releases before they're generally available to the public.

» **Training:** Gain access to free learning plans, best practices, and training modules.

» **Online and in-person events:** As part of the developer program, you're invited to ServiceNow developer events such as CreatorCon at the company's annual Knowledge Conference, as well as virtual and local events like hackathons, hands-on workshops, labs, meetups, and much more.

» **Community:** Get access to developer-oriented forums designed to help you build better apps. You can connect with and get guidance from other ServiceNow developers through online forums and in-person meetups.

Chapter 2

Storing Your Information

After you've planned your app (see Chapter 1), you're ready to build your data model. In plain English, that means you need to create one or more tables with fields in them, possibly loading the table(s) with data, and making sure the right people can access that data.

Getting to Know Your Toolbox

When it comes to storing your information, you have a few tools at your disposal in the Now Platform:

» **Studio:** Studio is a built-in way to keep track of your app's components (or files). Among developers, this is known as an integrated development environment (IDE). When you develop your app in Studio, you can test the app in another browser tab to speed up the build process.

» **Guided App Creator:** Guided App Creator is a wizard-driven experience that walks you through the initial process of building an app. You can import spreadsheets, create tables, define access, and configure multiple user interfaces in just a few minutes.

>> **Service Portal Designer:** Service Portal Designer allows you to create amazing web portals and pages that automatically adjust to desktop, tablet, or mobile devices.

>> **Flow Designer:** Flow Designer enables process owners to use natural language to automate approvals, tasks, notifications, and record operations without having to code.

Each of these tools is built into the Now Platform. They don't require any additional licensing.

TIP

Making Choices about Your Tables

ServiceNow offers three methods for creating tables (see Figure 2-1):

>> **Extending a table:** You can leverage an existing table to instantly create fields, logic, and more. This is a great way to accelerate your app creation.

>> **Uploading a spreadsheet:** Use the spreadsheet columns to define your new fields and, if you want, import the data.

>> **Creating a table from scratch:** You can build a new table and fields from the ground up. This method gives you total control over what information you want to store, but it may require a bit more work than the other two methods.

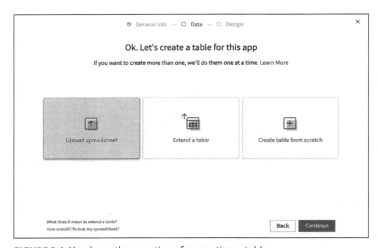

FIGURE 2-1: You have three options for creating a table.

REMEMBER

Uploading a spreadsheet is available only through Guided App Creator. Extending a table and creating a table from scratch can also be done in Studio.

WARNING

When you create a table from scratch, you can't go back and make it an extended table. Likewise, when you create an extended table, you can't "unextend" it later. If you made a mistake when you started out and you want to change it now, you need to create a new table and migrate your data.

If you have doubts about whether to create from scratch or extend, it's generally better to extend a table and not need the available fields and functionality than it is to realize down the road that you need them and you don't have them. Consider your options carefully before creating your data model and remember: Not every table should be extended from another table.

We cover each of these table creation methods in more detail in the following sections.

Extending a table

When you extend a table, your new table inherits all the fields and functionality from the table you're extending, saving you time. By far the most common table to extend in ServiceNow is the task table.

TIP

To determine if you want to extend a table, use the decision tree in Figure 2-2.

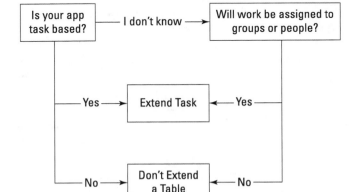

FIGURE 2-2: Extending a table can accelerate your app build process.

An additional, yet very important benefit of extending a table is roll-up reports. ServiceNow provides several tables already extended from the task table. Viewing data that all shares the same base (task) table is a no-brainer. A common example is when an employee wants to see all the work assigned to her. She only needs to look at the task table and filter on the Assigned To field to see tasks across multiple processes. Now you come along with a killer expense report app and choose to extend the task table. Automatically the expense reports assigned to an employee are added to the list of tasks without any additional work on your part. If you didn't choose to extend the task, employees would have to look at multiple lists from different tables to see all the work assigned to them.

If you determine from Figure 2-2 that extending an existing table is a good option for you, simply identify which table to extend and proceed to the next screen. From there, you can get familiar with which fields you inherited and add any fields you need to your new table.

TIP

When you extend a table, you have a number of fields to choose from (instead of creating new fields). Before creating a new field, check to see if there is an existing field that might meet your purposes simply by changing the field's label. Note that the purpose of the field should be similar to the purpose of the field in the base table.

Here are some examples of when you may want to extend a table:

>> **You have work that needs to be assigned to someone.** This would be a good time to look at extending the task table because it already includes fields to assign to a group and user.

>> **You have an asset that has similar, yet specific properties to something you already own.** Let's say you want to track tablets. They share many of the same fields as computers, but they have some unique aspects. Extending the Computer table would get you most of the fields you need to track tablets.

Uploading a spreadsheet

If you're creating an app based on a spreadsheet, each work-sheet is likely to map to a table in ServiceNow, each column may become a field in that table, and each row may become a record in that table (see Figure 2-3 and 2-4).

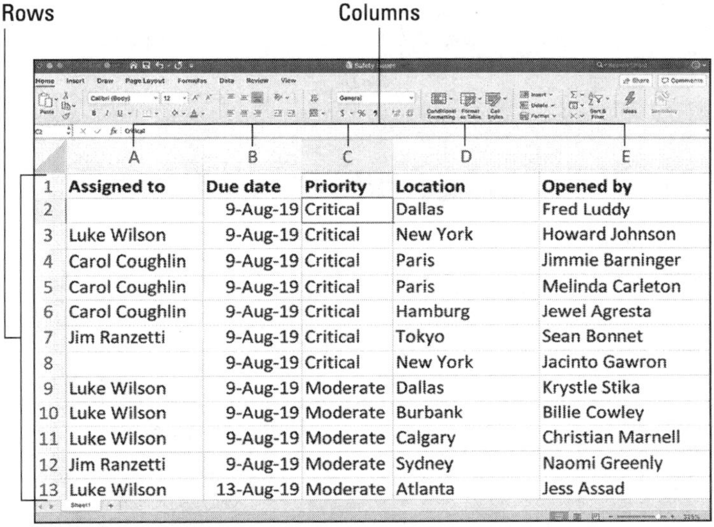

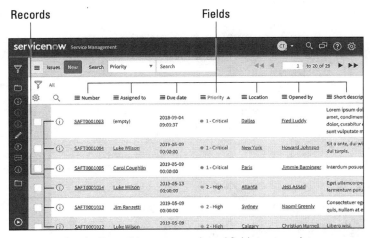

FIGURE 2-3: Spreadsheets contain rows and columns to store data.

FIGURE 2-4: ServiceNow tables use records and fields to store data.

Guided App Creator offers a step-by-step approach to import your spreadsheet. When you get to creating tables in Guided App Creator, simply click Upload Spreadsheet (refer to Figure 2-1), drag and drop your spreadsheet, define the field types needed (see the "Creating Fields" section later in this chapter), and, if you want, import the spreadsheet data. It's that simple.

REMEMBER

Guided App Creator only imports the first worksheet from the imported spreadsheet and expects the column headings to start in cell A1. If you need data from other worksheets or cells, take a look at Data Sources and Import Sets on the ServiceNow Product Documentation site (https://docs.servicenow.com).

Creating a table from scratch

Another option for creating a table is to create each field yourself. If you determined from Figure 2-2 that your best option is not to extend a table, then click Create Table from Scratch (refer to Figure 2-1).

The screen presents an interface that allows you to choose your field labels, types, and other properties, similar to the other two options to create the fields you need in your table. It's a lot like extending a table (covered earlier), but you don't get any existing fields.

Creating Fields

After you've created a table, you need to add fields to it. ServiceNow has many different field types with built-in validation. Choose the one that best fits that field's data type.

WARNING

You can easily make plain-text (string) fields where people can enter anything, but doing so can result in bad and inconsistent data that's difficult to use. For example, if you have a field on your table for someone's name, you use a plain-text (string) field and end up with data like you see in Figure 2-5. But if you use a reference field instead of a plain-text field, you get data that looks like Figure 2-6. Much better.

TIP

You can use reference fields to *normalize* (make consistent) your data by referencing an existing table in ServiceNow. ServiceNow has more than 2,000 tables at your disposal. The appendix lists some commonly used tables for building an app.

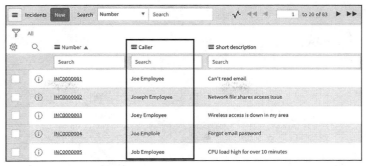

FIGURE 2-5: Using the wrong field type can lead to data inconsistency issues.

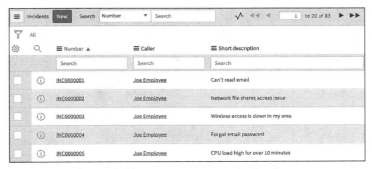

FIGURE 2-6: Reference fields are one way to standardize data.

A reference field can normalize your data, but other fields can be used for specific types of data. The complete list of field types can be found on the ServiceNow Product Documentation site (https://docs.servicenow.com), but Table 2-1 lists some common field types.

Choice fields versus reference fields

TIP

A common question among new builders is, "When should I use a choice field and when should I use a reference field if both are great for normalizing data?" Here are two questions to ask yourself:

» **How many options are you offering?** Use a choice field if your list of options is fairly short (say, less than 10 to 15 items). For example, you may want your user to pick a color. The list you propose contains values Red, Green, Blue, Yellow, Orange, and Silver. That's perfect for a choice field.

TABLE 2-1 Commonly Used Field Types

Field Type	Notes
Integer	A freeform input field that accepts number values only. Use this field type if the value will always be a number and you may be using it in calculations.
Currency	A freeform input field with a currency type. Use this field type when dealing with money.
Phone number	A combination of drop-down list to select country format and freeform input for the number. Use this field type when you need to validate phone numbers.
Reference	A record picker. Use this field type when you want to reference a record from another table.
Choice	A drop-down list. Use this field type when you need a short list of options to present to the user.
Date	A date picker. Use this field type if you don't need a specific time.
Date/time	A date/time picker. Use this field type if you're comparing specific times or the exact time is important.
String	A freeform text field. Use this field type if no other field type fits your purposes.

If your list has more than 15 items, you're probably better off with a reference field, so you don't cause the user to have to scroll forever. Reference fields make the user experience better in this case by offering a type-ahead feature. For example, in a list of names, if the user starts typing "br," she may be presented with options for Brad Tilton, Brett Oliver, and Brian Murray; then she can choose the correct value. The user can also use the magnifying glass icon to bring up a list and, optionally, filter to choose a name from that list.

» **What are your data values?** In the preceding example of colors, the option for Red may actually contain a value of #FF0000. This relationship is fairly clear.

Unlike choice fields (which offer one option to one value), reference fields can have additional information related to the displayed choice. The user would still pick Red from a list of car colors, for example, but the related record would have much richer information. For example, a value of #FF0000, a default distributor, pricing information, and more.

Field attributes

Each field can have various attributes. Some attributes are based on the field type, and others are common to all fields. Be sure to review the field types to determine if you want the field to be read-only, to be mandatory, to contain a default value, and more. How you set your field attributes can make a big impact on how users interact with your app.

TECHNICAL STUFF

Six fields are auto-created for every table in ServiceNow (see Table 2-2). They contain auto-populated information about the table, like when it was created, when it was last updated and by whom, as well as a unique identifier for the table. These fields cannot be manipulated.

TABLE 2-2 Default Fields in ServiceNow

Field Name	Database Name	Description
Created by	sys_created_by	The user who created the record.
Created	sys_created_on	The date/time that the record was created.
Updated by	sys_updated_by	The user who last updated the record.
Updated	sys_updated_on	The time the last record was updated.
Sys ID	sys_id	The unique identifier for the record. This is auto-assigned and unique throughout the instance.
Updates	sys_mod_count	The number of times this record has been updated since the record was created.

Putting the Finishing Touches on Your Tables

Creating a table is much like picking out a car — you may have your mind set on a make, model, and perhaps a color, but have you considered the accessories like the tires, the stereo system, the engine size, the interior style, the electronic gadgets? If you choose wrong, some of these can be swapped out or upgraded later, but others are permanent and you're going to have to live with them.

With tables, it's much the same. This section explains some of those check boxes, drop-downs, and other fields you encounter when you create your tables.

Choosing a table label

The table label is used wherever someone interacts with a list or record for your table. Some options include the left navigation menu, at the top of a list or record, or in a pick list of tables. The table label is modifiable (and translatable) after your app is created.

Picking a table name

The table name is the database name. It's typically not displayed to your end users, but it's the way in which ServiceNow interacts with the database. The table name is also prefixed with the app scope name.

TIP

Consider table names carefully. After the table name is created, you can't change it, so we encourage you to review your table names before saving so they make sense later. If you have an app called Loaner to manage your loaner items and you create a table called Loaner Request, the default table name may be something like x_snc_loaner_loaner_request. Before you save your table, consider modifying the table name to x_snc_loaner_request. You, or your developers, will appreciate this if you need to add scripting to your app later.

Making your table extensible

You can make any table you create capable of being extended to other tables simply by checking the Extensible check box.

Let's say you're building an app to track vehicles. These vehicles could be anything from cars to trucks to electric bicycles. The vehicles have a certain number of common attributes like owner, number of wheels, date of purchase, color, and so on. These fields could be put in a base table that you later use to extend to other tables with specific attributes (or fields) of their own. For example, number of doors would be applicable to cars and trucks, but not bicycles or motorcycles, so that wouldn't be a good candidate to put on your base table.

Auto-numbering your records

Auto-numbering allows you to add a sequential number to your record with a prefix. This prefix acts as a unique, human-readable designator so you can quickly find the record later. By checking the Auto-Number box when you create your table, you tell the system to create a field called Number with an associated character prefix and counter that gets automatically incremented with each new record.

Consider an app that tracks safety issues. It's much easier for someone to call in and refer to SAFT0010022 than it is to try searching for "that thing that happened in the break room where the wire wasn't plugged in to the doohickey."

REMEMBER

Not all tables need auto-numbering. The most common use of auto-numbering is for task-based records. Records that support a process (such as lists of people, locations, groups, or devices) are typically not auto-numbered.

Managing access

The final step in creating a table is to create and apply the roles identified earlier to establish what those roles can do to the records on your table.

There are four types of access: create, read, write, and delete. Each role you create may have different access. Consider granting the appropriate access based on the personas, or roles, your app requires. For example, you may want a user with an approver role to your app to have read and write access, but not create and delete access, whereas a user with an employee role may need to create as well as read and write.

WARNING

Use delete access with caution. Deleting records is normally not something you want to do, because it can leave gaps in your data. Consider using an active field to simply deactivate records you no longer need.

IN THIS CHAPTER

» **Getting to know the classic user interface of forms and lists**

» **Giving your users a mobile experience**

» **Providing your fulfillers and agents with a workspace**

» **Creating custom portals for your end users**

» **Working with reports and dashboards**

Chapter **3**

Creating Amazing Experiences

ow will people interact with your application? The Now Platform offers several ways to allow your users to interact with your app. There are standard forms and lists, a native mobile application, a custom portal, and a more recent user interface (UI) that ServiceNow simply calls *workspace.* Each has its own merits and is well suited for a specific type of persona or the work he or she typically does.

Will your app be accessed via desktop or mobile? Is your target audience already using an application on ServiceNow where they're comfortable using forms and lists, or will they need a self-service type of interface? Will they be doing quick updates on the go, or do they work in ServiceNow the majority of their workday? These are the design considerations when building an app for specific audiences. This chapter has you covered.

Using Forms and Lists

The standard method of accessing data in ServiceNow is through the default forms and lists. You may also hear this referred to as the "classic UI." A form displays information from one record in a data table, and a list displays a set of records from a table.

When configuring forms and lists there are a few guidelines you should follow:

>> **Keep the number of fields on a form to a minimum.** The more fields you have on a form, the longer it will take to load. Generally, users don't want to work with a long form either. You can use form views to create different sets of fields for different situations.

>> **Use form sections to logically group fields together and keep users from having to scroll.** The top section of the form should contain the fields that are always needed or used, while the other form sections contain less frequently used fields.

>> **Make sure fields appear in a logical order.** For example, a start date field should always come right before an end date field.

>> **Use seven or fewer columns in a default list.** People can add more columns if they want to by personalizing their lists. As tempting as it is to put a lot of fields on a list, users will have to scroll horizontally to see the "missing" columns, and that's just not a good experience.

>> **Avoid using a reference field as the first item in the list view, because it's shown as hyperlinked text.** Clicking the reference field redirects the user to the referenced record instead of the list record and results in a poor user experience. For example, when viewing a list of case records, the expectation (based on the way the majority of lists are configured) is to click the first column. If your list is different, in that it takes the user to the case owner instead of the case details, that's off-putting for the user.

Figure 3-1 shows an example of a poorly designed form. It's poorly designed because it has the following characteristics:

>> There are no sections — it's one long form.

>> Fields that don't require much space, like the date fields at the bottom, are taking up the full width of the form.

>> The left and right sides of the upper form feel unbalanced with more items on the right than the left.

>> Similar fields aren't grouped together (for example, "assignment group" and "assigned to" are on different sides of the form).

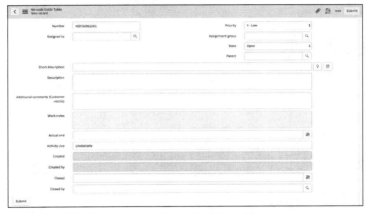

FIGURE 3-1: Nobody wants to use a poorly designed form.

By contrast, Figure 3-2 shows a well-designed form. It's well designed because it has the following characteristics:

>> Fields are grouped together logically, like "assignment group" and "assigned to."

>> Fields that don't take much space (date, choice, and reference fields) are placed side by side.

>> Short fields are balanced left and right where possible.

>> The form has been broken into sections for easier viewing and data entry.

FIGURE 3-2: Good form design can unlock productivity.

Taking It Mobile

ServiceNow offers native mobile capabilities for Android and iOS users. If users require functionality like geolocation or offline access to your data, you can use one of the two native ServiceNow apps: Mobile Agent, for the agents and fulfillers, and Now Mobile for your end users (see Figure 3-3). The development is done by creating a mobile application in Studio inside of the application you've been building. You don't need to learn iOS or Android development tools. The Now Platform takes care of the hard part, allowing you to focus on the logic and presentation of your app.

If you use Guided App Creator to get your app started, clicking the mobile option allows you to easily create a mobile experience simply by choosing tables. You can also create mobile apps manually using Studio to allow users to interact with your data.

TIP

What makes a good mobile experience? Mobile apps aren't designed to be a mobile version of all desktop functionality. The best mobile experiences come from quick interactions. When creating a mobile experience, keep the actions simple to allow users to create and update records. Think about the mobile apps you use the most to hail a ride or shop online. You open the app, you make your request, and you're done in a few minutes. The idea of mobile is to make it quick and easy. Some people have referred to this as a *targeted micro-experience.*

TIP

Individual applets can be secured by role, as well as made available in offline mode.

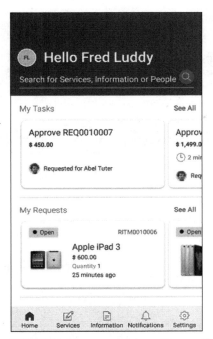

FIGURE 3-3: Access your data on the go with a mobile app.

Working with Workspace

You may find yourself with users of your app who practically live in ServiceNow to do their daily jobs. We refer to these users as *agents*. Agents may be people who fulfill requests, respond to cases, or address inquiries — theirs is a life of constant data flow. To make their jobs easier, ServiceNow offers Workspace (see Figure 3-4).

Workspace is a configurable service desk application that provides agents with an integrated and graphically intuitive user experience.

Workspace features include

>> A multi-tab interface to manage multiple cases or incidents
>> Real-time handling of calls and chats via the Interaction Management System

>> Task resolution assistance via Agent Assist

>> Intuitive search capabilities to quickly find relevant content

>> Heads-up display of contextual information to quickly get oriented to new tasks

By default, Workspace is active for all instances.

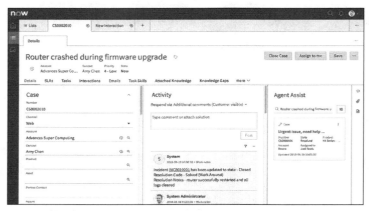

FIGURE 3-4: Easily manage multiple interactions with Workspace.

Getting the Ultimate Control with Service Portal

If during the planning phase, you decided that your application has a Requestor or Self-Service user, you may want to use Service Portal to provide a friendly web experience.

In order to give self-service users the ability to easily create records from your company's existing Service Portal, create a record producer from the table record (see Figure 3-5). A record producer provides a better end-user experience over a regular form by only presenting fields needed to get the process started instead of bogging them down in something more like a tax form. Talk to your ServiceNow Administrator about the appropriate catalog and categorization so the record producer is accessible through your Service Portal.

Alternatively, you may need to create a new Service Portal for your app if one or more of the following are true:

- » You need to provide different branding, navigation, or user experience than your organization's current Service Portal.

- » You need more control over branding and themes than the default (classic) interface provides.

- » Your organization does not have an existing Service Portal.

- » You need to provide more functionality than the portals included by default provide.

- » You need a more customized user experience than the default forms and lists can provide.

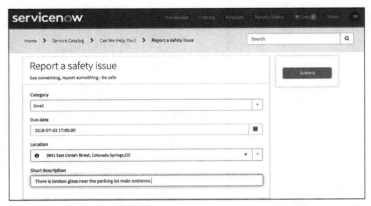

FIGURE 3-5: Record producers and Service Portal can provide a consumer-like experience.

TIP

If you find you need to create a new portal, avoid reusing any existing Service Portal pages in your app. Instead, create a new portal and new pages, and then reuse components in your pages like widgets and headers.

Using Reports and Dashboards

TIP

Most applications will have some level of reporting requirements. Reports should be created with actions in mind and be built to drive change. The reporting tool in ServiceNow is very powerful and easy to use. You can start by simply clicking a list column heading to make a bar or pie chart or use the wizard interface to guide you through more complex options (see Figure 3-6). With great power comes great responsibility.

Here are some guidelines to follow when creating reports:

>> **Be careful when reporting on large tables — it could have a performance impact on your ServiceNow instance.** Make sure you're filtering by date range or another limiting criteria rather than showing all records in the table.

>> **When grouping records in a report, try to avoid grouping by fields that contain many possible values — it could impact performance.**

>> **If running your report gives you a Long Running Transaction Timer message and takes a long time to run, consider adding more data filters to reduce the report run time.**

>> **If someone needs a report daily or weekly, consider scheduling it to be sent via email.**

The Now Platform reporting capabilities offer a wide variety of report types from simple bar graphs to heat maps to geographical maps. When you view a report in ServiceNow, the data is live — you can click a column in a chart and instantly view the underlying records that make up that data. This is far more advantageous than exporting data to a third-party application.

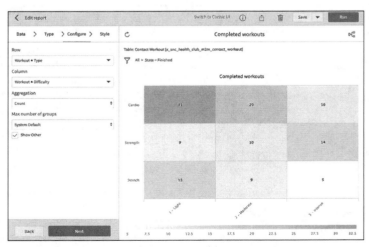

FIGURE 3-6: The built-in report builder offers a wizard experience for easy report generation.

You can also use dashboards to show multiple reports on one page (see Figure 3-7). Be careful with the number of reports you add to a dashboard. If you have too many reports on a dashboard and multiple users are using that dashboard, it could affect overall instance performance.

FIGURE 3-7: Dashboards are a useful way to group your reports and gain quick insights.

IN THIS CHAPTER

» Guiding your users with form logic

» Validating user inputs to prevent data issues

» Building more complex process flows

» Integrating your app to external systems

» Sending notifications at key process points

Chapter **4**

Logic and Workflow

After you've created your application's data model and provided your users a way to access the data, you're ready to add some logic. Logic is what makes your app a useful tool. It can come in many forms, ranging from *form logic* (what people can and cannot see or use on a form) to *business logic* (rules that govern what happens to data after it's entered) to *notifications* (making users aware of conditions and events within the app). Logically, this section covers logic.

Building Dynamic Form Logic

Controlling what users see when they visit a form can greatly increase productivity and responsiveness. For example, users should only see fields that are useful to them and they may need to see different fields based on what they've selected so far. Several options exist for controlling what's visible, read-only, and mandatory on a form, as well as showing conditional messaging.

The following question will help direct you to the right decision for when to control user access to information: Is this a suggestion or enforcement?

A suggestion makes the form easier to complete, whereas enforcement forces the user to do something in order to complete the form.

TIP

User interface (UI) policies are useful for conditional suggestions like showing and hiding fields or adding field messages based on another field's value, while data policies and business rules are better suited for doing conditional enforcement like making a field mandatory.

Figures 4-1 and 4-2 show an example of a UI policy in action. When the category is set to Big (see Figure 4-1), the Due Date field is displayed and mandatory (note the asterisk to the left of the Due Date field). When the category is set to Small (see Figure 4-2), the form automatically updates to hide the Due Date field.

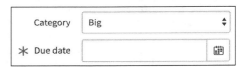

FIGURE 4-1: A UI policy checks the value of the category and displays the due date when the category is Big.

FIGURE 4-2: The same UI policy hides the due date when the category is Small.

TIP

The best user experience happens when you utilize both suggestion and enforcement together.

Validating and Simplifying Updates with Business Rules

Business rules are logic and validation rules that run when a record is created or updated. They're good for building simple conditional logic to run after the form is submitted, like this:

Trigger: *If* this happens on a record,

Action: *then* set this value or show this message.

As an example, let's define a business rule to validate that the due date entered was not in the past. The trigger could be that the due date has changed and the date is at or before the current minute. This is easy to construct using the condition builder like the one shown in Figure 4-3.

FIGURE 4-3: Use the condition builder to easily construct business rule triggers.

If the user enters a date in the past, then the trigger condition is true. It displays a message and stops processing as defined on the action part of the form (see Figure 4-4).

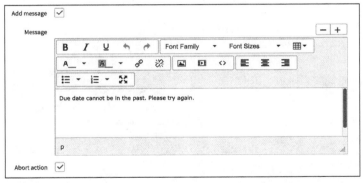

FIGURE 4-4: Update record field values or display a message and stop processing.

More complex logic with multiple steps can be done via Flow Designer.

Controlling Your App with Flow Designer

Flow Designer allows you to build powerful business workflows. When designing a flow, keep the following tips in mind:

>> Each flow should have a singular goal.

>> Use sub-flows to create reusable components in a flow (approval is a great example).

>> The layout of your flow should clearly indicate its purpose. If there is confusion, consider adding annotations (comments) to the actions.

Start with a whiteboard design of your business flow. Then build the flow, action by action, to align with your process. You may need more than one flow for a single process to stick to the tips we just mentioned.

A basic flow consists of a trigger with one or more actions and logic; it may call a sub-flow. The trigger tells the flow when to start. Flows can be triggered in one of the following three ways:

>> **Record created, updated, or both:** A record on the designated table has been created, updated, or both. You may have certain requirements where you want your flow to trigger on specific conditions for new or updated records. For example, only start an approval on an expense report when the state changes to approval. A condition can be applied to the trigger to filter which record actions can trigger the flow.

>> **Scheduled:** Run a flow once or on a repeating interval. One example is to find all requested approvals that have not been updated in the last week and send a reminder notification to the approvers.

>> **Application:** On a new ServiceNow instance, the default for this option is Service Catalog. This means you can define a flow to be triggered by a specific catalog item. Let's say you have a service catalog item to grant entitlements to a user account. When the user clicks the Order button, you can launch a flow for that item that retrieves and uses variables specific to the catalog item, gets approvals based on those

variables, and updates the access records. See how easy automation can be?

Flow Designer actions are the part of the flow that *do* something (for example, send an email notification, update a record, look up records, or create new records).

Flow Logic can be applied to make decisions about the data in your flow. There are several logic choices, including "if" (see Figure 4-5) and "decision tree" to conditionally determine whether to run a set of actions (or not), looping constructs like "for-each" and "do-until" to iterate on a list of items like records from a lookup action, or just tell your flow to hang out and wait a certain amount of time.

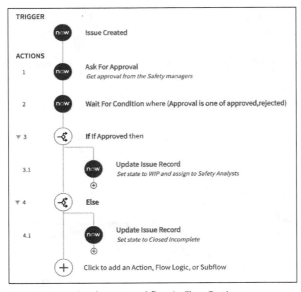

FIGURE 4-5: A simple approval flow in Flow Designer.

Sub-flows allow you to create reusable blocks of actions. For example, let's say your flow automatically approves and updates a record if the amount is less than $1,000 but requires manager approval for amounts greater than $1,000. You're going to need to do the same update twice in that flow: once when the system auto-approves and again if the manager approves. Why create two sets of the same actions when you can create a sub-flow containing the approval actions and drop it in twice? You've made your flow easier to read and easier to maintain. Experience has taught us that requirements change. When someone asks you to update the approval action, you only have to update it once instead of twice because you've isolated that part of the logic in a sub-flow.

Check out Flow Designer on the ServiceNow Product documentation site (`https://docs.servicenow.com`) and look at some example videos on the ServiceNow YouTube channel (`https://youtube.com/user/servicenowdemo`).

Connecting to Third-Party Systems with IntegrationHub

If your app needs to send or receive information to a third-party system, you're going to need an integration. Fortunately, you can use Flow Designer using prebuilt integration actions from IntegrationHub. In Flow Designer, you simply select from available IntegrationHub bundles of actions called *spokes* (see Figure 4-6) while building a flow to easily allow ServiceNow to interact with other systems in your application landscape. For example, if your team uses Slack for collaboration, you can have your flow send a notification automatically to a Slack channel. For the available spokes in your organization, contact your ServiceNow System Administrator.

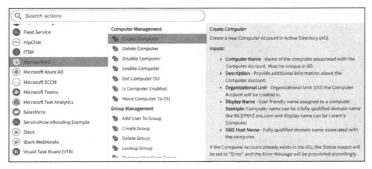

FIGURE 4-6: Connecting to third-party systems is done using IntegrationHub.

TIP

Additional spokes are available from the ServiceNow store (`https://store.servicenow.com`). People with some coding and integration skills can also build new spokes. If a particular integration is not available from ServiceNow, this may be an opportunity to work with your organization's professional developers to build a custom, reusable spoke for that particular system.

Using Notifications to Communicate

Most applications need some sort of email notifications configured. Some examples of that are

>> When a task is assigned to a user or group

>> When a request is opened or closed on behalf of someone

>> When an approval is needed from someone

There are many examples already in the notification table you can use if you need to create your own notifications. It's very easy to copy those and change the copies to suit your purposes.

Configuring notifications is quite easy. You only need to identify when to send the notification, who will receive the notification, and what the notification will contain (see Figure 4-7).

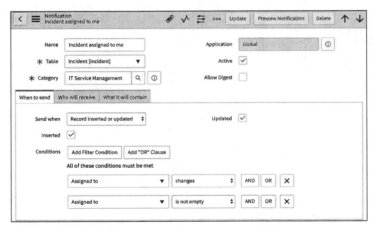

FIGURE 4-7: Use notifications to keep others informed at key points in your process.

Here are some tips for working with notifications:

>> **Consider keeping the Send to Event Creator check box unchecked.** In this case ServiceNow will not send an email to the person who took the action causing the email to be sent. For example, if I assigned a task to myself, I don't need to be notified about it.

>> **Use email templates if you think you'll be sending out multiple notifications containing the same subject and/ or body.** For example, if you're sending an email when a task is assigned to a group, it'll probably contain the same text as an email getting sent to the assigned user, even though the conditions and recipients will be different for both notifications.

>> **Instead of specifying a specific user or group (also known as *hardcoding*) in a notification, consider using the notification record field labeled Users/Groups in Fields to automatically use the data in the user or group reference field from your app's data record.** This is also one more reason to use a reference field over a string field in your table.

IN THIS CHAPTER

» **Adding a chatbot**

» **Testing your app**

» **Using surveys**

» **Offering online tours**

» **Enhancing navigation**

Chapter **5**

More No-Code Capabilities

n this chapter, we explore some additional no-code capabilities of ServiceNow that you can use to enhance your app and the user experience. You aren't required to use any of these capabilities in your app, but it's great to know what they are and the value they can add.

Building a Chatbot

If your app has one or more high-volume/low-complexity tasks, you may want to consider a chatbot. Virtual Agent is a conversational bot platform for providing user assistance through conversations within a messaging interface. Use Virtual Agent to build bots and design bot conversations that help your users quickly obtain information, make decisions, and perform common work tasks.

Components of Virtual Agent

The Virtual Agent platform includes the following components:

>> **Virtual Agent conversational (client) interface:** With Virtual Agent, your users interact with a chatbot or live agent through various messaging services. Your users can use the web-based Virtual Agent interface available for Service Portal, Apple iOS, and Google Android environments. They can use the Virtual Agent interface for third-party messaging applications through the ServiceNow integrations for Slack, Microsoft Teams, and Workplace by Facebook.

>> **Virtual Agent Designer:** Use Virtual Agent Designer to develop, test, and deploy bot conversations that assist your users with common issues or self-service tasks. Virtual Agent Designer is a graphic tool for building the dialog flows of bot conversations, called *topics*. A topic defines the dialog exchanged between a virtual agent and a user to accomplish a specific goal or resolve an issue.

Predefined topics are available for Customer Service Management (CSM), HR Service Delivery, and IT Service Management.

>> **Live agent handoff (see Figure 5-1):** Give users the option to switch to a human agent for assistance during bot conversations. Virtual Agent is integrated with live chat to offer a seamless transfer from a bot conversation to a live agent. With live chat, you specify the agent chat queues to be used, including the chat interactions transferred from a virtual agent to a human agent. Your users can request a live agent transfer at any time during a chatbot conversation. You can also initiate a live agent transfer through custom conversation flows that you build.

Benefits of Virtual Agent

Implementing a virtual agent to handle common requests and tasks enables your users to get immediate help, day or night. Providing your virtual agent on channels familiar to your users, such as third-party messaging apps, offers a convenient way for them to get work done quickly. A virtual agent can also offer personalized customer experiences by applying and remembering user information during the conversation.

FIGURE 5-1: You can give users self-service capability and handoff to a live agent as needed with a chatbot.

Typical Tier 2 support tasks that can be accomplished with virtual agents include

>> Answering frequently asked questions

>> Providing tutorial ("how to") information

>> Querying or updating records (for example, getting the current status of cases or incidents)

>> Gathering data, such as attachments, for the live agent

>> Performing diagnostics

>> Resolving multistep problems

Automating these support tasks with a virtual agent frees your support agents to focus on more complex user issues and enables you to scale your support organization accordingly.

You can access Virtual Agent Designer in ServiceNow by choosing Collaboration ⇨ Virtual Agent ⇨ Designer. Take a look and see if your process, users, and app can benefit from a conversation with a chatbot.

Testing Your App

Before deploying your app to production, your IT or app development group may require you to build a test to ensure its functionality and avoid surprises down the road. Even if they don't require a test, it makes sense to invest a few minutes to validate your app.

Automated Test Framework (ATF) enables you to create and run automated tests to confirm that your instance works after making a change. The change could be a ServiceNow change (something ServiceNow does) or an application configuration change (something you do). If everything tests positive (see Figure 5-2), you can make the changes to production with confidence. If you run in to issues, use the test results to identify changes needing review. You can find ATF under the Automated Test Framework menu.

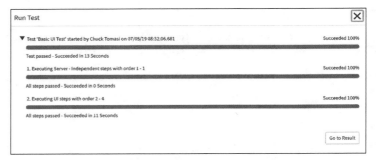

FIGURE 5-2: Validate a release and speed up upgrades with the click of a button with ATF.

Components of the Automated Test Framework

Understanding the components of ATF can help you build more effective and easy-to-run tests. A *test* is made up of steps you define. These include things like opening a form, filling in fields, and validating results. You can run each test individually or as a collection called a *test suite.* Test suites are typically grouped together functionally. For example, if your app is fairly simple, you could have a test suite for your entire app and test it with one click from the test suite.

Benefits of the Automated Test Framework

Automated Test Framework provides the following benefits for change managers and builders/developers:

>> Reduce upgrade and development time by replacing manual testing with automated testing.

>> Design tests once and reuse them in different contexts and with different test data sets.

>> Keep test instances clean by rolling back test data and changes made after each test runs.

>> Create test suites to organize and run tests in batches.

>> Schedule test suite runs.

>> Enable non-technical test designers to create tests of standard Now Platform functionality.

>> Reduce test design time by copying quick start tests and test suites.

>> Create custom test steps to expand test coverage.

We like to say that ATF tests are the gift that keeps on giving. Once defined, they can be used to validate your app releases and also have a bonus when it comes to upgrading your instances. Your tests are already defined and ready to go. At the push of a button, you can validate your app quickly and get the value of ServiceNow's latest releases faster!

Sending Surveys

With the ServiceNow Survey Management application (see Figure 5-3), you can create, send, and collect responses for basic surveys. The survey designer lets you create survey categories and questions, configure the details, and publish the survey to specific users or groups.

You can assign a survey to individual users or groups who receive all the questions from all the categories. You can also customize each question and make it dependent on the response to another question. The following describes the procedures you follow to create and publish a survey.

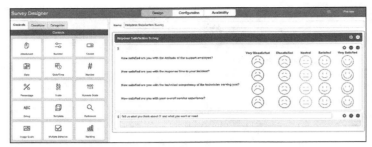

FIGURE 5-3: Create and configure surveys using the Survey Designer.

1. **Create survey categories.**
2. **Create questions within each category.**
3. **Configure survey details, such as introductory and closing remarks and time limit.**
4. **Select recipients for the survey.**
5. **Publish the survey to the selected users or groups.**

Surveys can be a useful metric to determine if your app is successful. You can find surveys under the Survey menu on the right navigation menu in ServiceNow.

Offering Self-Paced Onscreen Training

Guided tours help train and onboard users within the ServiceNow user interface (UI). Each tour contains a series of interactive steps that help users complete online tasks within the browser window. Administrators can create tours for ServiceNow applications, service portals, and custom applications (see Figure 5-4). For example, you can create a tour to represent a training model for specific policies and processes, such as creating a new claim or reviewing expense reports.

Guided tours use a series of steps that may span multiple pages. You can create purely informational steps that users read through and acknowledge, which results in no change to the ServiceNow instance. Alternatively, you can provide users with an interactive experience where they click through and actively work with the application at hand. For example, an Introduction to Incidents tour may simply show them the key features of the Incidents table, while a Create Your First Incident tour may actually walk them through creating a real incident, which results in a new record in the Incidents list.

FIGURE 5-4: Use the Guided Tour Designer to create tours that demonstrate how to use a feature.

A guided tour can accelerate adoption of your app and reduce supplemental training and documentation. You can find guided tours under Guided Tour Designer on the left navigation menu.

Improving Standard Menus

As part of the application creation process, you most likely built a table or two. Whether you did this in Guided App Creator, in Studio, or directly from the left menus, ServiceNow probably created a menu option for your app as well as a submenu item (known as a *module*) for your users to access a list of records in your table. Although this is a great start, you may find you need additional navigation options to allow users quick access to your data, including the following:

>> **Prefiltered lists to allow users to quickly access a subset of records in your table(s):** With one click, you might get them to all open records, all closed records, or records assigned to the person logged in. This is the most common type of module that builders add.

>> **A dashboard or homepage showing various reports.**

>> **A dedicated module to create a new record.**

>> **A collapsible separator between different groupings of navigation modules:** For example, you may have a separator between the general application data that have a high touch rate (open, closed, and all cases) and administrative records used less frequently to configure your application behavior (inspectors, locations, properties), as shown in Figure 5-5.

>> **A URL to an external page related to your app such as a third-party documentation site or map.**

TIP

As with most things when building an app, start simple and you'll know when it's time to add a module. Starting with too many modules can be daunting to someone just getting started. Secure your application menu and modules using roles to ensure proper access to the elements of your app.

FIGURE 5-5: Application menus and modules make a great way for users to access your data.

TIP

The easiest way to create and manage application menus and modules is within Studio.

Chapter **6**

Ten Tips for No-Code App Development

The tips in this chapter come from years of experience across hundreds of implementations by customers, partners, and ServiceNow developers. If you follow these ten tips when building your app, you'll be in a great place.

Making a Plan

When you begin with a plan, you have a clear picture of the outcome you're looking for and how to get there, and that means you have a greater chance of success (see Chapter 1).

Naming Apps, Tables, and Fields

As you build your data model, remember to consider good naming of tables and fields.

REMEMBER

Labels can be changed later, but names cannot (see Chapter 2).

Considering Some Common Personas and Roles

In most apps, there are several default roles to consider when you build your app. A user (or requester) role is often assigned to someone who typically creates the record, checks the status, and makes small updates on his own behalf. An admin is someone responsible for the management and maintenance of the app. We often see a role for someone responsible for interacting with the record to drive the process; this persona may have a name like agent or fulfiller. You may opt to create a separate role for an approver, who is only involved with a specific approval step in your app (see Chapter 2).

Using Good Form and List Layout

Consider the experience users will have as they interact with your app. Watch how they move through forms and lists. Are there common things they do and in a specific order? Can you adjust the layout to make it easier for them to navigate and perhaps save time? (See Chapter 3 for more information on paying attention to the user experience.)

Taking Advantage of Different Field Types

ServiceNow offers several different field types. Take a look at the options available and consider how they might make your app more effective. You may find that changing a date and time field to a date gives you better reporting capabilities or using a URL field instead of a text field allows users to click a link and be taken to that site. (See Chapter 2 for more on field types.)

Avoiding Deleting Records

As a general rule of thumb, deleting records is bad because it can lead to data inconsistency issues. A better method is to add a True/False field (often called Active) to enable you to deactivate records like those of former employees. Then, when you use a reference field to those records, you can use a filter to retrieve just the active records.

Testing Your App

Use Automated Test Framework (ATF) to create tests for your app. Remember to use both good test cases (where you expect it to pass) and bad test cases (where you expect it to fail). When you use ATF, you can validate changes before going to production and reduce upgrade time between ServiceNow versions (see Chapter 5).

Getting Familiar with the Commonly Used Tables

Review the list of commonly used tables in the appendix. Understanding the built-in tables can save you development time, reduce the need for integrations, and improve cross departmental workflow (see the appendix).

Limiting the Number of Records Retrieved in a Report

More data equals more time. If you find your dashboards, reports, or lists are taking an uncomfortable amount of time to display, consider adding filters such as "created today" or "assigned to me" to reduce the amount of data retrieved (see Chapter 3).

Working with Your Developers

ServiceNow is a single development platform that accommodates all developer skill levels. This enables more people to build using no-code capabilities, leveraging the developer skill set as needed.

TIP

If you find your app needs complex logic or custom integrations that go beyond the no-code capabilities, work with the developers in your organization. The result is less backlog for the developers and faster throughput for you.

Appendix

Resources

We recommend the following resources for further information on ServiceNow no-code app development:

- » **ServiceNow documentation:** The ServiceNow docs site (https://docs.servicenow.com) has full documentation to the various platform capabilities mentioned in this book.

- » **ServiceNow developer portal:** The developer portal isn't just for hard-core developers. As a no-coder, there is plenty for you! Get a free ServiceNow personal developer instance, helpful videos, online learning plans, and more at https://developer.servicenow.com.

- » **ServiceNow community:** If you find yourself in need of help, there are thousands of subject matter experts in the ServiceNow community (https://community.servicenow.com), eager to offer help on a variety of topics.

Finally, Table A-1 lists the commonly used tables in ServiceNow.

TABLE A-1 **Commonly Used Tables**

Label	Name	Description
User	sys_user	List of all ServiceNow instance users.
Location	cmn_location	List of all user locations. Users are typically associated with a location.
Group	sys_user_group	List of all the groups. Users are typically associated with groups and inherit any security roles associated with those groups.
Company	core_company	List of companies that interact with your organization.

(continued)

TABLE A-1 *(continued)*

Label	Name	Description
Role	sys_user_role	List of security roles in the instance. Some will be default roles; others will be created by your organization.
Task	task	The common base table that gets extended. It has fields and functionality related to assigning work across teams and individuals, managing the state or the task, and other functions.

Notes

Notes

Notes

Notes